The Awesome Boss Playbook: 10 Strategies for Leading with Style

Marako Marcus

Published by Marako Marcus, 2024.

Copyright Page

While every precaution has been taken in the preparation of this book, the publisher assumes no responsibility for errors or omissions, or for damages resulting from the use of the information contained herein. No part of this book may be reproduced, stored in a retrieval system, or transmitted in any form or by any means, electronic, mechanical, photocopying, recording, or otherwise, without the prior written permission of the publisher, except as permitted by applicable copyright law. The information and views expressed in this book are those of the author and do not necessarily reflect the views of any organization or entity. All names, characters, and incidents in this book are fictitious. Any resemblance to real persons, living or dead, is purely coincidental.

The Awesome Boss Playbook: 10 Strategies for Leading with Style

First Edition, December 1, 2024.

Copyright © 2024 Marako Marcus.

Written by Marako Marcus.

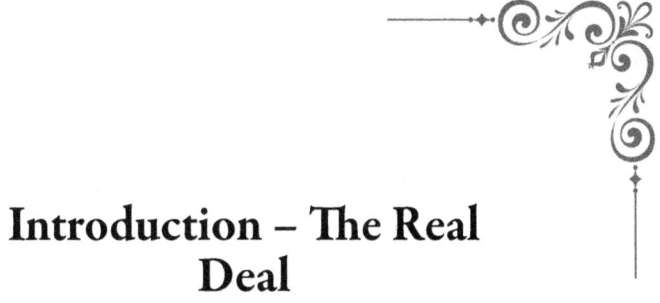

Introduction – The Real Deal

Let's get straight to the point. This book isn't some regurgitated AI-generated, textbook stuff. These strategies? They're not just a collection of feel-good theories or shiny buzzwords. They come from 25+ years of getting my hands dirty, facing the tough calls, working with the real leaders and the not-so-great ones. I've watched teams thrive and crash, bosses succeed and fail, and everything in between. This is the unfiltered truth about what it takes to be an awesome boss.

I've worked with companies big and small, from the Fortune 500s to local startups, and what I've learned is this: leadership isn't some mysterious art that's reserved for the chosen few. It's a skill—one you can learn, practice, and master. You don't need a PhD in leadership. You need the guts to make the hard decisions, the clarity to lead through chaos, and the humility to build a team that thrives even when you're not in the room.

Take Mandy, for example. Mandy's been leading a mid-sized tech team for five years. When I first met her for our coaching sessions, her team was struggling. Overworked, underappreciated, and morale in the gutter. If you'd asked me what I thought of her leadership, I would've said she was in over her head. She didn't have the right tools. She was playing it safe. She thought leadership was about being the smartest person in the room, about having all the answers.

But that wasn't the problem. The problem was she wasn't leading her team—she was just managing them. She was stuck in a cycle of micromanagement, endless meetings, and giving feedback that didn't cut to the heart of the issue. That's when we had a conversation. I told her to stop being the bottleneck. I told her to stop pretending that she had to have all the answers. I told her she needed to stop hoarding the spotlight. Mandy didn't need to be a hero. She needed to be the lighthouse. She needed to create an environment where her team could step up and shine.

Fast forward six months. Mandy shifted gears. She started applying the strategies I'm about to lay out for you. She hired smarter people, got out of their way, stopped pretending she had all the answers, and started being a guide, not a roadblock. The change was immediate. Her team became more innovative. They started solving problems on their own. They stopped waiting for her to give them permission to take risks. And, more importantly, they delivered. The company turned around. Revenues improved. She didn't just help the company—she built a team that was strong enough to succeed without her constant oversight.

And that's what this book is about. It's about being the best leader you can be, in your own style, with your own unique strengths. It's about understanding what makes a leader great and then taking action—simple, actionable steps—to get there.

Now, let me walk you through the 10 strategies that helped many leaders. These are strategies you can start using today.

1. Be the Lighthouse, Not the Spotlight

Stop hogging the limelight. Your team doesn't need another hero. They need a guide. Be the steady force that helps your team navigate through rough waters. The spotlight should be on them, not you.

2. Hire Smart, Then Get Out of Their Way

Hiring the best talent is the easy part. The real challenge? Letting them do their thing. Empower, don't micromanage. If you hire someone better than you in their area, then step aside and let them work their magic.

3. Say It Like You Mean It

Straight talk. No corporate fluff. People don't trust bosses who beat around the bush. Say what you mean, mean what you say, and make sure everyone knows where they stand.

4. Feedback: Give It, Take It, Love It

Feedback is the lifeblood of growth. Don't just give it—learn to take it too. If you can't handle criticism, you've got a problem. Leaders grow by giving honest feedback and taking it like a pro when it's directed at them.

5. Celebrate Wins, Fix the Fails

When your team crushes it, celebrate like you're at the Super Bowl. When they fail, own it, learn from it, and move on. No blame games. Real leaders take responsibility and focus on the future, not the past.

6. Master the Art of the Coffee Chat

If you don't know what drives your people, you're not leading, you're managing. Get to know your team on a personal level. Skip the generic "How's it going?" and dig deeper. You can't lead people you don't understand.

7. Be the Calm in the Chaos

When everything's going to hell, your team looks to you. Don't freak out. Stay calm, stay focused, and show them how to handle stress like a pro. You're not a leader if you panic when the heat is on.

8. Decisions: Make Them, Own Them

Indecision is the death of leadership. You can't afford to sit on the fence. Make decisions, stand by them, and own the consequences. If they're wrong, fix them and move on. Leadership is about action, not hesitation.

9. Lead Like a Human, Not a Robot

You're not a machine. Show some emotion. Admit when you're wrong. Crack a joke. Be real. People follow leaders they can relate to, not robots who speak in corporate jargon.

10. Build Leaders, Not Followers

Your job isn't to create a fan club. Your job is to create other leaders. Teach your team to think critically, take initiative, and lead with integrity. Your legacy will be the leaders you build, not the tasks you complete.

These are the strategies that will change the game. Forget the corporate nonsense, the leadership models, the cookie-cutter advice. This is the real stuff. The stuff that works.

So let's get to it. You ready to become the leader you were meant to be? Let's go.

Strategy 1 – Be the Lighthouse, Not the Spotlight

Let me say it as it is: leadership isn't about you. It's not about how much praise you can rack up or how many awards you can collect. It's about guiding your team to success. You're not there to be the hero. You're there to make sure the team doesn't drown when the storm hits. When shit hits the fan, the best leaders are the ones who stand tall in the background, steady and unshakeable, while their teams do the heavy lifting. They don't hog the spotlight. They are the lighthouse, not the ship.

Why does this matter? Because leaders who can't let go of the limelight will never create high-performing teams. You've got to be the one who's always there when the team needs direction, but never the one to claim the credit. Your job is to create an environment where the team feels empowered, capable, and confident enough to make decisions without needing to ask for your permission every step of the way. But you've got to trust them first.

Here's a hard truth: people don't follow bosses who make everything about them. They follow those who make it about the team. The moment you start trying to be the star of the show, you're sending a message that you don't trust your people. And that's a toxic message. When your team feels like they're only there to make you look good, they won't put their best foot forward. Why should they? They're not the ones getting the praise—they're just the ones carrying your baggage.

I've seen it time and time again: leaders who love the spotlight, love taking credit for everything that goes right, but when things go wrong, they point fingers and disappear into the shadows. Those leaders burn out their teams. They create resentment. They build cultures of fear. And that fear isn't from the challenges of the job—it's from the toxic, self-centered leadership they're forced to endure.

Let's talk about Mandy again. When I started working with her, she was stuck in the spotlight. She was trying to do everything herself—taking credit for the wins, answering every question, solving every problem. It wasn't because she was a control freak (well, not entirely), it was because she thought that's what leadership was supposed to look like. She believed she had to have all the answers, that the buck had to stop with her.

The more Mandy took the spotlight, the less her team was willing to take risks. They weren't stepping up. Why would they? Mandy was already "handling it." She was the one speaking in meetings, making the decisions, and taking the praise. Why would they stick their necks out? Why would they own a project when she was already there, stepping in to take the credit?

The moment Mandy made the shift to become the lighthouse, everything changed. She started letting her team lead. She started recognizing their accomplishments. She stopped solving every problem. Instead, she guided the team with clear direction, provided the tools they needed, and got out of the way. She made it clear: "I trust you. You've got this." That shift in mindset—stopping the pursuit of glory for herself and shining the light on her team—was a game-changer.

If you're sitting there thinking you can lead by staying in the spotlight, you're wrong. You're not leading. You're micromanaging. You're not guiding, you're suffocating. Leadership isn't about being the center of attention. It's about being the steady force that provides clarity and direction. When the storm is raging, people need a lighthouse, not a captain who insists on steering the ship even when they're not the best person for the job.

The problem is, a lot of bosses think leadership means taking control of everything. They're afraid to delegate because they fear losing credit, and they're afraid to trust because they don't want to look weak. But in reality, not trusting your team is the only thing that makes you weak.

Being a boss who hogs the spotlight is the easiest path to mediocrity. You might look impressive in the short term. You might get a few pats on the back. But if your people aren't stepping up to the plate, if they're not owning their roles and solving problems on their own, you're not building a great team. You're building a dependency. And in a fast-paced, ever-changing world, that dependency is your downfall.

Your role as a leader isn't to be the best at everything. Your role is to surround yourself with people who are better than you in key areas and give them the space to do what they do best. You're there to provide the vision, the strategy, the direction—but your team will do the heavy lifting. When they succeed, they succeed because of their own hard work, not because you swooped in to save the day. And when they fail? That's on you. You're the lighthouse. You provide the steady hand when things go wrong, but you never throw your people under the bus. You show them how to learn, how to pivot, and how to come back stronger.

But this isn't just about your team—it's about you, too. You need to let go of your ego. Stop measuring your worth by the amount of recognition you get. Your value as a leader isn't found in the number of awards you collect or the number of "atta boys" you receive. It's in the success of your team. When your people succeed, that's your win. When they fail, that's your lesson.

The best leaders aren't the ones who take all the credit. They're the ones who make sure their teams succeed, whether they're standing at the front or standing in the back. They don't need the spotlight. They need results. And when their team thrives, so do they.

Being the lighthouse means being a consistent presence, a guiding force. It means knowing when to step forward and when to step back. It means trusting your team to do the work, but also making sure they have everything they need to succeed. It's the most powerful leadership move you'll ever make.

So ask yourself this: Are you leading like the lighthouse, or are you still fighting to be the star of the show?

Strategy 2 – Hire Smart, Then Get Out of Their Way

Seriously, if you're still playing the role of the boss who does everything and controls everything, you're missing the whole point of leadership. Your job isn't to be the expert in everything. It's to build a team of experts. Your job is to hire the right people, give them the tools they need to do their jobs, and then—here's the kicker—get out of their way. That's it. It's that simple.

The most common mistake I see with bosses? They think leadership is about being the smartest person in the room, the one who has all the answers. They believe that by holding onto every little decision, by putting their fingers in every pie, they're adding value. In reality, they're suffocating their team. You can't lead like that. You're not a bottleneck, you're the fire extinguisher. If you're slowing down progress or micromanaging every detail, you're failing your team, not leading them.

Let's break it down. You can't do it all. No matter how skilled you are, you cannot excel in every aspect of your business. If you try to, you'll burn out. Your team will burn out. And nothing will get done at the level it needs to get done. This is where hiring smart comes in.

Hiring the right people is the foundation of a successful business. But here's where most bosses screw it up: they hire based on gut feeling or an unproven track record. They look for people who will just "fit in," who will do what they're told, and who will serve as a mirror image of themselves. If you're doing that, stop. You're creating a team of clones, not a powerhouse.

The key is to hire people who are better than you in their areas of expertise. Find the people who have the skills, the passion, and the drive to take your team to the next level. And don't just hire the ones who make you feel comfortable. Hire the ones who challenge you. Hire the ones who will push you to think differently, who will make you uncomfortable. You need diversity—diversity of thought, experience, and approach. That's how you grow. That's how you scale.

Once you've got the right people in place, the next step is even more critical: you need to get out of their way. Give them the freedom to operate. Give them the trust to make decisions. You've already hired them for their expertise, so now it's time to let them do their jobs. Trust them enough to know they don't need you hovering over their shoulder every second.

Here's the hard truth: if you're micromanaging, you're part of the problem. You're undermining your team's confidence. You're sending the message that you don't believe in their abilities, that you don't trust them to handle things on their own. And that's toxic. People can only grow and develop if they're given the opportunity to do so. If you're always there making every decision for them, you're holding them back. You're creating dependency, not independence.

I'll tell you a story about Mandy again. When I first started the coaching sessions with her, she had a hard time letting go. She was one of those leaders who needed to have her hand in everything. She thought she had to approve every email, make every decision, and double-check every report. She was working 16-hour days, completely burned out, and frustrated that her team wasn't stepping up. Why? Because she wasn't giving them the space to do so. She was choking the life out of them by not trusting them enough to handle their own work.

It wasn't easy for Mandy, but once she made the switch, everything changed. She started letting go of the small stuff and giving her team the space to succeed. She trusted them to make decisions, and most importantly, she got out of their way. She gave them room to take ownership of their roles, make mistakes, and figure things out. And guess what? They rose to the occasion. The team started taking initiative. People were solving problems on their own. The results were better, the morale was higher, and Mandy found herself with more time to focus on strategy and growth.

What happened next? Mandy's business grew because her team started growing. They were empowered to take ownership of their work. They were solving problems, improving processes, and coming up with new ideas. She was no longer the bottleneck. The business was moving faster, and it was moving in the right direction. It wasn't just because Mandy was a great boss; it was because she got out of the way and let her team take the reins.

So why do bosses struggle with this? Because they're afraid. They're afraid that if they let go, the team will fail, and they'll look bad. They're afraid that by letting others make decisions, they'll lose control. But here's the thing: control is an illusion. You can't control everything. You can't control every outcome. What you can control is how much trust you give your team. You can control how much space you give them to thrive.

Letting go doesn't mean you abandon your responsibility. It doesn't mean you stop providing direction, guidance, or support. It means you stop getting involved in every little detail. It means you trust your people to handle what they're good at and focus on the bigger picture. When you do that, you'll see a transformation in your team. You'll see them take pride in their work, own their decisions, and rise to challenges.

So here's the challenge for you: Stop trying to be the hero. Stop trying to micromanage every detail. Stop trying to solve every problem yourself. Hire people who are better than you in their areas of expertise, and then give them the freedom to shine. Your job is to trust, guide, and empower. Their job is to deliver. And when you get this right, you'll be amazed at how much more your team can achieve.

You can't lead from the front if you're too busy doing everyone else's job. Hire smart, then get out of the way. Let your team lead the charge. That's how you build a winning team. That's how you build a lasting legacy as a leader.

Strategy 3 – Say It Like You Mean It

If you want to be an awesome boss, you've got to speak like you mean it. No more corporate-speak, no more trying to sound polished, no more beating around the bush. Straight talk is the only talk that works. Don't sugarcoat the truth. Don't dance around difficult conversations. And for God's sake, stop using meaningless jargon to sound important. Your team will see right through it, and they'll start tuning you out.

The problem with most bosses today is that they're afraid to be direct. They're scared of conflict, terrified of hurting someone's feelings, or worried that being blunt will make them seem unapproachable. So, they hide behind vague phrases and empty platitudes. "We need to improve," they say. "We need more collaboration," they say. "Let's do better," they say. Guess what? Those words mean nothing. They're a waste of breath. If you want to get anything done, if you want to lead your team, you need to be crystal clear and stop wasting time.

Here's what being direct really looks like: It means telling your team exactly what you expect from them. It means giving them honest feedback, even when it's tough to hear. It means calling out bad behavior or poor performance immediately. It means not being afraid to ruffle feathers when it's in the best interest of the team and the organization.

Now, I get it. You're probably thinking, "But I don't want to come off as harsh." Here's the deal: Being direct isn't about being rude. It's about being respectful. You're not being an asshole when you say what's on your mind clearly and honestly. In fact, the opposite is true. When you avoid the hard conversations or soften the truth, you're disrespecting your team. You're saying, "I don't think you can handle the truth." And that's not leadership—that's babying your team.

Let me give you a real-world example. A few years back, I worked with a leader named David. David was a senior manager in a growing tech company, and his biggest issue? He just couldn't say what he really meant. David spent hours in meetings saying things like, "We need to think about this," or "Let's explore this idea some more." It was code for, "I'm not sure what I want," or "I'm avoiding making a decision."

As a result, his team had no clarity on what they were supposed to be doing. They were left second-guessing every direction he gave. His team wasn't failing because they didn't have the skills. They were failing because they didn't know what the hell they were supposed to do. And David? He wasn't doing them any favors by dancing around the hard truths. He was just creating confusion and frustration.

Finally, I told David, "You need to stop being vague. You need to speak directly, even if it's uncomfortable." And let me tell you, he hated that advice. He was scared of how his team would react if he suddenly stopped softening his words. But he trusted me enough to try it. He started cutting the irrelevant stuff out of his communications. He became more direct in his feedback. If something wasn't working, he called it out immediately, no beating around the bush. The change was immediate. His team started to respond with more confidence. They weren't guessing anymore. They were getting clear, actionable direction from their leader, and they performed better because of it.

Now, here's the truth most bosses won't tell you: Being direct means you have to take responsibility for your words. You have to own the impact of what you say. That means you can't hide behind vagueness when you screw up. You can't give a half-assed apology when you don't follow through on something. And you can't blame your team when things go wrong. When you screw up, you own it, and you say it like you mean it.

THE AWESOME BOSS PLAYBOOK: 10 STRATEGIES FOR LEADING WITH STYLE

Take Mandy, for example. When she first started getting direct with her team, she made a lot of mistakes. There were a few occasions where she gave feedback that didn't land well, or she spoke in a way that wasn't as tactful as it should've been. But instead of avoiding responsibility, she addressed it head-on. She said, "Hey, that feedback didn't come across the way I intended, and I want to clear that up." She didn't make excuses. She didn't try to cover it up. She took responsibility and clarified her message.

When you speak directly and own your words, people start to trust you more. They start to see you as someone who isn't afraid of difficult conversations. And that trust? That's what makes you an awesome boss. When your team knows you'll always tell them the truth, even when it's tough, they'll start to follow you with loyalty. They'll respect you because they know you're real with them, not just putting on a show.

But don't make the mistake of thinking being direct is just about delivering bad news. You also need to give credit where it's due. Praise people publicly when they do something great. Don't leave it to the grapevine. When someone kicks ass, tell them exactly why they kicked ass, and make sure the whole team knows it. Straightforward praise builds morale and motivates people to keep doing their best.

So, here's what you need to do:

1. Stop hiding behind vague statements. Tell people what you really mean.
2. Be honest in your feedback. If someone's underperforming, tell them. If they're doing great, tell them.
3. Own your words. Take responsibility for what you say, especially when you screw up.
4. Don't be afraid to ruffle feathers. If you need to challenge someone, do it. If you need to push back on an idea, do it. If something isn't working, say it.
5. Praise openly and specifically. Let people know when they've

done a great job, and make it clear why you're acknowledging them.

Being an awesome boss isn't about making everyone feel good all the time. It's about being real. And if you can't handle being real, you'll never be the leader you're capable of becoming. Speak like you mean it, and your team will start to take you seriously. You'll earn their respect, and you'll build a culture of transparency, accountability, and trust. That's how you lead with power. That's how you become an awesome boss.

Strategy 4 – Feedback: Give It, Take It, Love It

If you're not giving feedback, you're failing as a boss. If you can't handle feedback, you're failing even harder. And if you're not encouraging a culture where feedback is welcome and embraced, you're pretty much setting your team up for mediocrity. Feedback isn't a "nice-to-have" component of leadership. It's the very lifeblood that fuels performance, growth, and accountability. If you aren't making feedback part of your daily routine, you're missing the point of leadership.

Too many bosses think feedback is a once-in-a-while thing. They do it in formal reviews, in quarterly sit-downs, or when it's "convenient." But that's not enough. Feedback should be coming in real-time. It should be continuous. It should flow in both directions, up and down the hierarchy. And it should never be treated like a chore. If you want to be an awesome boss, you need to embrace feedback like it's your job to give it, take it, and thrive on it.

You know who gets this? Cynthia. Cynthia is one of the best managers I've ever coached, and it's because she doesn't just talk the talk when it comes to feedback—she walks the walk. Cynthia has a simple philosophy: feedback is how we grow. She gives it, takes it, and loves it. She doesn't fear it, and she doesn't shy away from it. She sees it as an essential part of leadership—something that sharpens her skills and helps her team level up.

Cynthia shared that she had a team member, John, who wasn't performing well. Now, most bosses would either ignore the problem or drop the hammer with harsh criticism. But Cynthia didn't do that. She sat down with John and gave him honest feedback. "You've got potential, but you're not hitting the mark right now. Here's what needs to change." And then, after giving him the feedback, she asked for his feedback. "What do you think I could do to help you be more successful?" She didn't pretend to have all the answers. She was willing to listen and adapt. And you know what? It worked. John turned things around. Why? Because he knew exactly what was expected of him, and he had the support he needed to succeed.

You can't just drop feedback on people and walk away. If you want to get the most out of it, you need to follow up, provide support, and make sure that the feedback sticks. That's how you build trust. That's how you build a team that's continuously improving. When feedback is a regular part of your leadership style, your team gets better every single day.

But let's talk about something that's even more crucial: being able to take feedback. No one likes to be told they're wrong, but guess what? It's a reality of leadership. You can't grow if you don't hear the truth about yourself. If you can't handle feedback, you're not ready to lead. It's as simple as that.

I've had bosses who couldn't take criticism, and it was painful to watch. They would deflect, deny, or even retaliate. It created a toxic environment where no one wanted to speak up, and no one grew. Being able to receive feedback without flipping out, without getting offended, without making excuses is a sign of real leadership maturity. When you show your team that you're open to hearing what they think about your leadership, you give them the confidence to speak up. You show them that their voices matter, that their input is valuable. And that's the kind of culture that makes people want to follow you.

Let's face it, feedback isn't just for the big moments. It's not just when someone's doing great or when someone's screwing up. It's for every little interaction, every tiny detail that can make a difference. If you see someone handling a situation well, tell them. Don't wait for the annual review

THE AWESOME BOSS PLAYBOOK: 10 STRATEGIES FOR LEADING WITH STYLE

to acknowledge their hard work. If someone's dropped the ball, call them out immediately. Don't wait for the quarterly meeting to address the issue. Timing is everything. Be timely with your feedback, and don't let issues fester. Don't let praise go unsaid. Your feedback will be far more effective if you're giving it regularly, consistently, and with intent.

And here's another truth most bosses won't admit: feedback is often uncomfortable. Giving it can be uncomfortable. Taking it can be uncomfortable. But guess what? That discomfort is where the magic happens. If you're not uncomfortable with feedback, you're not doing it right. The discomfort means growth. It means you're pushing yourself and your team to become better. If you want to build a culture of accountability, excellence, and continuous improvement, then get comfortable being uncomfortable.

Let me be clear: feedback is not about being nice. It's not about being polite. It's not about avoiding confrontation. It's about being real. It's about helping people see the truth, even when it's tough to hear. And it's about helping yourself see the truth, even when it's hard to accept.

So, what do you need to do to make feedback work for you?

1. Give it often: Don't wait for the quarterly review or the annual meeting. Give feedback every chance you get. Celebrate the wins, and address the problems as soon as they arise.
2. Be specific: General praise is nice, but it doesn't help anyone grow. Be specific in your feedback. "Great job on the project" doesn't tell anyone what they did right. "Your attention to detail in this project was excellent. You caught issues early, and your solutions were spot-on" is what makes someone feel seen, appreciated, and motivated.
3. Ask for it: Never stop learning. If you're not getting feedback, ask for it. Regularly ask your team what you can do to be a better boss. It'll show them that you value their input and that you're committed to being a better leader.

4. Take it without defensiveness: When you get feedback, listen carefully. Don't justify, don't explain. Just listen and learn. The best leaders are the best listeners.
5. Follow up: If you've given feedback, follow up. Don't leave people hanging. Check in to see how they're doing, offer guidance where needed, and make sure they know you're there to support their growth.

Feedback isn't a one-time thing. It's a culture. If you want to be an awesome boss, you need to create a feedback-rich environment where everyone—yourself included—is growing and improving every single day. You need to embrace it, love it, and make it a priority. And that, my friend, is how you build a high-performing, motivated team that will follow you to the ends of the earth.

Strategy 5 – Celebrate Wins, Fix the Fails

People don't give a damn about your boss title if you don't know how to show up for them when things are good—and when things go south. The role of a leader isn't just about pushing people to work harder, faster, smarter; it's about showing up for them when it counts. It's about being the first to celebrate victories and the first to take ownership when things go wrong. That's how you build respect. That's how you build trust.

Let me give you an example—let's talk about Mandy again. She's got this incredible ability to celebrate every win, big or small. I've watched her run teams through hell, juggling deadlines, budgets, and expectations—and when they hit a milestone, she's the first one to acknowledge it. She doesn't just say "Great job," and call it a day. No, she gets specific. "You guys nailed this project. The way you handled X, Y, and Z was brilliant. I couldn't have done this without you." That kind of recognition makes people feel seen, valued, and energized. It reminds them that their hard work matters. And let me tell you—people go harder when they know their contributions will be acknowledged. You can't fake it, though. If you aren't genuinely celebrating, your team will see right through you. It's about being real, and Mandy is real. Her enthusiasm is contagious.

The best bosses don't just celebrate the wins. They fix the fails. And that's where a lot of bosses mess up. The moment something goes wrong, they're nowhere to be found, or worse, they point fingers. Blame games?

Those are for amateurs. Real leaders own their part in the failure and focus on fixing what went wrong. They don't let problems fester, and they don't shy away from the hard conversations.

I've seen too many managers who are great when things are going well but fall off the face of the earth when problems arise. Their response? Avoidance. They sweep it under the rug, hoping it will resolve itself. But guess what? It won't. Problems don't just disappear because you ignore them. They grow. They fester. And if you don't face them head-on, they'll come back to haunt you. As a boss, your job is to confront failures, fix them, and make sure everyone learns from them. No one is perfect, and that includes you.

Mandy has this down to an art. Last year, one of her projects went completely sideways. A major client was unhappy, and the team's performance was slipping. Most bosses would have tried to throw someone under the bus. But Mandy took responsibility. She didn't deflect. She didn't pass the blame. She brought the team together, had an honest conversation, and said, "We messed up. Here's what went wrong, here's what we're going to do about it, and here's how we're going to make it right." She didn't sugarcoat the situation, but she also didn't let anyone feel alone. She kept everyone in the loop, kept them focused on solutions, and most importantly, she led the charge in making things better. And because she did that, the team rallied around her. They didn't see her as a boss who avoided failure—they saw her as a leader who faced it head-on and guided them through it.

Let's break it down. The way you celebrate wins and fix fails can make or break your leadership credibility.

If you're not celebrating your team's successes, you're missing a massive opportunity. People want to know that their hard work counts. They want to feel like they're part of something bigger than themselves. Recognition fuels motivation. But this isn't just about giving out high-fives at the end of a project. It's about acknowledging effort, progress, and growth.

THE AWESOME BOSS PLAYBOOK: 10 STRATEGIES FOR LEADING WITH STYLE

The key here is to be specific. Don't just say, "Good job, everyone." Get into the details. If someone stayed late to get the job done, acknowledge that. If someone came up with a creative solution that made a difference, give them credit. Celebrate milestones. Celebrate the small wins, not just the big ones. It builds momentum. When people know their effort is recognized, they're more likely to put in the same level of commitment in the future.

And here's the thing: your celebration doesn't have to be some grand event. It can be a simple thank you. It can be a shout-out in a team meeting. It can be a quick email that says, "You killed it this week." People want to be seen, and you have to make the effort to see them.

Now, let's talk about what happens when things don't go as planned. Failure is inevitable. You can't avoid it. But what you can do is take ownership of it. Your team isn't going to trust you if you pass the blame. If you point fingers, if you throw someone else under the bus, you're going to lose their respect. Own your failures. Acknowledge what went wrong and, more importantly, fix it.

When something goes wrong, don't shy away from the tough conversations. Gather your team, discuss what happened, and figure out what you can do differently next time. Lead by example. Don't let failure define you or your team. Use it as a stepping stone for growth. Make sure everyone is on the same page and focused on what needs to happen to get things back on track.

Here's an example. One of the teams I worked with had a major project that fell behind schedule. The client was angry, and morale was low. The team was looking for someone to blame. But the leader, let's call her Laura, didn't point fingers. Instead, she said, "Okay, let's figure out what went wrong and how we can fix it. We're not going to let this slide. We're going to learn from this, and we're going to do better next time."

Laura didn't dwell on the failure. She didn't let it consume the team. She gave them the space to learn, to grow, and to adapt. And that's the difference between a leader who builds trust and one who destroys it.

Celebrate the wins, and fix the fails. But make sure you're doing both with intention. Recognition should be about more than just saying, "Good job." It should be about making people feel seen and valued for the effort they put in. And when things go wrong, don't run away from the problem. Fix it. Take responsibility. Learn from it. Your team needs you to be the steady hand in the storm, guiding them through both the victories and the setbacks.

You can't be a boss who only shows up when things are going well. You need to be there when things fall apart too. Lead with humility. Lead with transparency. Lead with the commitment to fix what needs fixing. And you'll have a team that will follow you through thick and thin.

Strategy 6 – Master the Art of the Coffee Chat

Leadership isn't about sitting in the corner office barking orders. It's about people. And the best way to understand your people, to know what makes them tick, what drives them, and what makes them want to leave the company, is through the simplest, most underappreciated tool in your leadership toolkit—the coffee chat.

If you're not having regular, honest conversations with your team members, you're already behind the curve. The coffee chat is where the magic happens. It's where trust is built, where you connect on a human level, and where you learn what really matters to your people. Forget the fancy performance reviews, forget the KPI tracking. Get real with your people. Find out what keeps them up at night, what they care about, and what they think about the direction of the company. If you aren't doing this, you're missing a major opportunity to lead with impact.

Now, you might be thinking, "I don't have time for casual chit-chat. I'm busy managing the team, driving the business forward." Yeah, I get it. But guess what? If you're not taking time for these casual, "non-work" conversations, you're failing as a leader. Simple as that. If you're only meeting with your people when it's time to review performance or discuss results, you're missing the most important part of leadership. People don't open up in structured meetings. They open up when they feel comfortable, when they know you care, and when they know you're not just trying to "manage" them. That's what a coffee chat is all about.

Let me hit you with a real example here. Remember Mandy, the leader I mentioned earlier? She gets it. She's not the type to sit in her office all day and only talk to her team during scheduled meetings. She's always out there, grabbing a coffee with someone from the team. It's the 10-minute, off-the-cuff conversations that build the real relationships. I've seen her pull someone aside in the hallway, offer a genuine "How's it going?" and then dig deeper, asking about challenges, ambitions, and frustrations.

Let me tell you, those 10-minute coffee chats aren't just nice-to-haves for her—they're essential to the way she leads. She learns what's working and what isn't. She knows who's feeling disengaged and who's stepping up as a potential leader. She gets insights into her team's mindset and can course-correct when things start to go off track. And that's why she has such a loyal, motivated team. They don't just see her as a boss—they see her as someone who cares. They see her as a leader who's willing to listen and connect. They trust her, because she shows up for them. That's how trust is built. Through genuine connection. Through real conversations that go beyond the surface.

But let's not sugarcoat things here. These coffee chats aren't about exchanging pleasantries. They're not about surface-level "how's the weather?" nonsense. If you want to be an awesome boss, you have to dig deeper. You need to be asking questions that matter. You need to know what your people care about, what they're struggling with, and what's motivating them—or, more often, demotivating them. You've got to be prepared to ask tough questions, listen, and truly hear the answers. If you're not asking about what's really going on in your people's heads, you're just going through the motions.

Here's what a coffee chat should *not* look like:

1. It's not about small talk: I get it, you don't want to dive straight into heavy stuff. But don't hide behind pleasantries. Don't waste time on "How's the weather?" or "Have you seen the

latest movie?" Get to the heart of the matter. Ask questions that give you insight into the person's world. Ask about their challenges, their career goals, their frustrations. Make it real.

2. It's not a one-way street: The goal isn't for you to just talk at them. It's about listening. This is where you learn. This is where you listen for what's *not* being said. If someone's disengaged, it's not always going to be obvious. You have to read between the lines. You have to listen to what's unsaid, what's left out, what's missing. Your job is to figure out what's really going on—and that means hearing more than just the words coming out of their mouth.

3. It's not a performance review: The coffee chat is not a place to grill your team members about KPIs or project timelines. If you try to make every conversation about results, you'll get nothing. People will stop being open with you. The coffee chat is about them as humans—not just as employees. It's about connection, not critique.

Here's what a good coffee chat looks like:

1. Be curious: Stop assuming you know everything about your people. Ask questions. Let them talk. What's really going on in their life? What challenges are they facing? What's exciting them about the future? What keeps them up at night? You can't lead people if you don't understand them. And you can't understand them if you don't ask the right questions.

2. Listen: The art of a good coffee chat is listening—really listening. Don't just wait for your turn to talk. Don't just nod and wait for the conversation to end so you can get back to "real work." The coffee chat is your time to truly hear your people. Pay attention to their tone, body language, and what's *not* being said. People give off clues all the time—you just have to be paying attention.

3. Follow up: A great leader doesn't just have one coffee chat and move on. You've got to follow up. If someone tells you they're struggling with something, ask them about it next time. Show them that you care. Show them that you're invested in their growth, not just their output.
4. Be vulnerable: If you want people to open up to you, you've got to be willing to open up yourself. Share your own struggles, your own challenges, and your own wins. Vulnerability is a two-way street. When your people see that you're human too, they'll feel more comfortable sharing with you.

Coffee chats are the most underrated leadership tool, and you can't afford to ignore them. If you want to be an awesome boss, you need to connect with your team on a personal level. That doesn't mean pretending to be their best friend. It means showing them that you care about more than just their work output. You care about *them*. And when your people know that you see them as real people—not just as resources—you'll have their loyalty. You'll have their trust. And that's what makes a boss truly awesome.

So, go ahead. Schedule that coffee chat. Get out of your office. Ask real questions. And listen. That's the kind of leadership that wins hearts, minds, and results.

Strategy 7 – Be the Calm in the Chaos

If you want to be an awesome boss, you've got to master one thing above all else: the ability to stay calm in the chaos. And let me be blunt—this is where most bosses fail. When the pressure's on, when deadlines are tight, when the team is panicking, when everything seems like it's about to go off the rails, the true leaders rise. And guess what? It's not the ones who are screaming, running around in a frenzy, or looking for someone to blame. No. It's the ones who can stay cool under pressure, think clearly, and lead their teams through the storm. That's what makes a boss awesome. That's what sets you apart from the noise.

When everything feels like it's falling apart, the worst thing you can do is add to the chaos. Your team looks to you for guidance. They're watching your every move, reading your body language, listening to your tone, trying to gauge your reaction. And if you lose it, they lose it too. If you panic, they panic. If you throw your hands up in frustration, they'll throw theirs up too. You've got to show them how to handle adversity—how to stay focused, stay productive, and most importantly, stay sane. You've got to be the rock. The calm in the storm. The steady hand guiding them through the mess.

Remember Mandy? Let me tell you about a time when things were spiraling out of control on one of her projects. There was a major issue with a client, and the team was freaking out. The pressure was on. Deadlines were tight. People were scrambling. It would have been easy for Mandy to lose her temper, to point fingers, or to start yelling at people to fix the problem. But she didn't. Instead, she took a deep breath, remained composed, and got her team back on track.

Mandy didn't try to sugarcoat things. She didn't pretend everything was fine. She acknowledged the situation for what it was: messy and high-pressure. But she didn't let that stop her from thinking clearly. She called a quick meeting, reassured the team that they could handle it, and gave clear, actionable steps to solve the problem. She was calm, collected, and in control—and that gave her team the confidence to get things done. The chaos didn't break her, and because of that, it didn't break the team. That's leadership.

So, what does it take to be the calm in the chaos? First of all, you've got to have emotional control. Your emotions are contagious. If you let stress or frustration show, it will spread. If you're snappy, tense, or visibly stressed, your team will pick up on it. And before you know it, everyone is on edge. You've got to own your emotions. Control them. When the pressure is on, your ability to stay calm will be the difference between success and failure.

Now, that doesn't mean you should bottle everything up and act like nothing is wrong. That's not the point. Emotional control means knowing when to take a step back, breathe, and give yourself a moment to think before reacting. It means not letting the moment control you, but controlling the moment. It means showing up as the person who's in control, who can think clearly and make rational decisions, even when everything around you feels like a disaster. That's how you set the tone. That's how you lead.

Second, you've got to focus on the solution, not the problem. It's so easy to get caught up in the drama, to dwell on what went wrong, to point fingers and assign blame. But that's a waste of time. You're the boss. Your job is to get things done, not to rehash mistakes. When chaos hits, your focus should be on fixing it. You've got to think about what needs to be done right now. What's the first step to resolving the issue? What's the next step? Break the problem down into manageable chunks, and then take action. Keep your eyes on the goal. It's easy to get stuck in a negative cycle when things go wrong, but the best bosses keep moving forward. They don't waste time lamenting the failure. They get to work fixing it.

Take Mandy's example. When her team hit that major obstacle with the client, she didn't waste time pointing fingers. She didn't get lost in frustration. She acknowledged the problem, but she immediately shifted the focus to solving it. What needed to be done? Who needed to handle what? What's the timeline? She gave clear instructions, kept everyone focused on the solution, and rallied the team around getting things done. That's what made her effective in that moment—her ability to take action instead of getting caught up in the problem.

Third, you've got to maintain perspective. When things are chaotic, it's easy to lose sight of the bigger picture. You start focusing on the immediate pressure, the urgency, the stress, and it feels like the world is crumbling. But a great leader doesn't get swept up in the chaos. They know how to step back and remember what's really important. In those moments, it's crucial to remember your purpose, your mission, and your goals. You've got to remind yourself and your team why you're doing what you're doing. What's the ultimate goal? What's the bigger picture here? If you're able to keep perspective, it'll be easier to stay calm and focused.

Finally, you've got to be a problem-solver, not a problem-creator. In a crisis, the last thing your team needs is someone who adds to the confusion. They need someone who can assess the situation, come up with solutions, and lead with clarity. This is where many bosses fail. They panic. They point fingers. They get bogged down in the details. They start blaming people, assigning guilt, and making it worse. As the leader, your job is to be the solution, not the problem. Your team needs you to be the one who provides clear direction, calm reassurance, and the right answers.

So, let's recap: To be the calm in the chaos, you've got to:

1. Control your emotions: Stay composed, breathe, and don't let

stress or frustration take over. Be the emotional anchor for your team.
2. Focus on solutions, not problems: Don't get stuck in the negative. Get clear on what needs to be done, and take action.
3. Maintain perspective: Don't lose sight of the bigger picture. Keep your eyes on the goal and keep the team focused.
4. Be a problem-solver, not a problem-creator: When the heat is on, you can't afford to add to the mess. Be the one who clears the way, not the one who adds to the confusion.

When you can stay calm under pressure, your team will look to you for guidance, trust you to lead them through tough times, and follow your example in handling future challenges. And that's what will make you an awesome boss. So, when the next storm hits, you better be ready to be the calm in the chaos.

Strategy 8 – Decisions: Make Them, Own Them

Here's the thing that most bosses don't get: if you want to be an awesome boss, you've got to make decisions. Period. No more hemming and hawing, no more sitting on the fence, no more endlessly debating. If you want respect, you've got to take action. You've got to make the call, even when it's tough, even when there's risk involved. An awesome boss doesn't hesitate. An awesome boss steps up, makes a decision, and owns it.

Let me be blunt: indecision is the death knell for leadership. It's like quicksand. The longer you stay stuck in it, the deeper you sink. The longer you avoid making decisions, the more people will question your ability to lead. You can't lead a team if you're constantly unsure of where you're going. If you keep pushing off the tough decisions, you're sending a message that you don't have confidence in your own judgment, and you're not capable of guiding your team to success.

I've seen it time and time again. A manager who can't make a decision. A leader who drags their feet. They talk a big game, they have all the theories, all the strategies, all the 'what-ifs,' but when it comes time to actually pull the trigger, they freeze. They stall. They wait. And while they're waiting, the rest of the team is getting frustrated. People start losing faith in their leadership. Morale takes a dive. People stop following, because why would they? If the leader can't make a damn decision, why should they?

But here's the thing: making decisions is hard. It's not easy. It's not comfortable. It means stepping into the unknown, dealing with uncertainty, and accepting that you don't have all the answers. But that's the price of leadership. You've got to take risks. You've got to make choices, even when there's no perfect solution. Because guess what? There will never be a perfect solution. There will never be a decision without consequences. But that doesn't matter. What matters is that you take ownership of the decision, and you stick with it.

Take Mandy again. She's been in situations where she had to make decisions that could have huge consequences. Previously, she would be holding back on making the decisions. After a few coaching sessions and some thought-provoking questions, she realized that she wanted everything to be in perfect order before making the decision. She decided then to develop herself to be more decisive.

The next time when she needed to make a tough call about whether to cut some of the budget or to pull back on a major project. It was a hard choice. There was no way to make everyone happy. Both options had risks. But Mandy didn't sit there paralyzed, waiting for someone else to make the call. She took the time to gather the data, consider the options, and then she made the decision. Was it hard? Definitely yes. Did she lose sleep over it? Of course. But she didn't avoid it. She made the decision, she owned it, and she led her team through it.

What's the key here? Confidence. You have to have the confidence to make decisions, even when you're not 100% sure you're right. A great boss doesn't wait until everything is perfect. A great boss makes decisions based on the information they have, their instincts, and their experience. Then, they commit. They go all in. They don't second-guess themselves every two minutes. They don't waste time wondering if they should have made a different choice. They made the call, and now they're sticking to it.

Now, I know what you're thinking: "But what if I make the wrong decision?" Great question. Let's talk about that. Guess what? You will

THE AWESOME BOSS PLAYBOOK: 10 STRATEGIES FOR LEADING WITH STYLE

make the wrong decision sometimes. It's inevitable. You're human. But here's the difference between a great boss and a bad boss: when a great boss makes a wrong decision, they own it. They don't hide from it. They don't blame others. They don't point fingers. They step up, acknowledge the mistake, and take responsibility. And then, they fix it. That's leadership. Taking ownership. Even when it sucks. Even when you're wrong.

And here's the thing: people respect a boss who owns their mistakes. They'll trust you more if you admit when you're wrong and work to fix it. Because let's be real—nobody expects you to be perfect. Nobody expects you to have all the answers all the time. But they do expect you to be honest. They expect you to make decisions and stick by them, even when the going gets tough. And when you admit that you were wrong, you've just earned a ton of respect.

The best bosses don't shy away from tough decisions. They make them, they own them, and they lead their team through the aftermath. They don't get stuck in analysis paralysis, worrying about every possible outcome. They take action. And when things go sideways, they fix it. Simple as that.

Now, let's talk about the most important part of this strategy: owning your decisions. This is where most bosses drop the ball. They make the decision, but they don't take ownership of it. They blame external factors, they make excuses, they act like they didn't have a part in it. And that's the kind of behavior that erodes trust and confidence. When you make a decision, it's yours. Own it. Don't deflect. Don't run away from it. Stand by it, learn from it, and move forward. When you own your decisions, you show your team that you're not afraid to lead. You're not afraid to take responsibility. And you're not afraid to step up when things get tough.

Being a great boss means making decisions and owning them. You don't have to be right all the time, but you do have to be decisive. You do have to be bold. You do have to show your team that you can lead with confidence, even when the road is uncertain.

So, what do you do now? Make a decision. Right now. Don't overthink it. Don't wait for the perfect time. Don't ask for a thousand opinions. Make the call. Commit to it. And then, own it. Because if you want to be an awesome boss, that's what it takes. Decisions. Action. Ownership. No more waiting around for someone else to step up. That's your job. Do it.

Strategy 9 – Lead Like a Human, Not a Robot

Leadership isn't about becoming some emotionless, robotic decision-making machine. It's not about presenting yourself as a flawless, distant figure who only talks in corporate jargon. If that's your idea of leadership, you might as well pack up your office now. You're not fooling anyone.

People follow leaders they can relate to, not leaders who come off like they're reading from a script. You can't connect with your team if all you do is preach about performance metrics, corporate vision, and leadership principles. You can't inspire people if you're too busy trying to be the perfect leader instead of just being a human. Leadership doesn't need to be a performance. It needs to be real.

I've seen leaders who try too hard to be this untouchable, superhuman figure. They maintain this stiff, corporate persona. Their emotions are locked up tight, their facial expressions are rehearsed, and everything they say is a calculated, polished statement. And you know what? It's exhausting. Not for them—because they're so busy being perfect—but for everyone else. Their teams start tuning out. They stop feeling like they can talk to them. And what happens next? They lose engagement. They lose trust. They lose respect.

Now, I'm not saying you need to go around crying at meetings or sharing your deepest, darkest secrets with your team. But come on, show some real emotion. People want to follow a leader who's human—someone who acknowledges their struggles, their triumphs, their imperfections. A real leader is someone who laughs at a funny joke, admits when they've made a mistake, and shows empathy when things go wrong. A leader who's willing to show up as themselves, not as a carefully constructed persona. That's leadership.

Why does leading like a human work? It's simple: people want to connect with people. They don't want to work for a robot. They don't want to be cogs in the machine of some distant, unemotional corporate entity. They want to feel seen. They want to feel heard. They want to know that their leader has the same struggles, the same worries, the same ambitions. If you can't do that, you're not leading—you're managing, and there's a world of difference between the two.

I'll tell you a story about one of the most effective leaders I've worked with, a woman named Sarah. She's a CEO who built an incredible company culture from the ground up. What made Sarah different from other bosses I've worked with? She was unapologetically human. She was real. She didn't hide behind a corporate mask. She showed up every day as Sarah—the person, not the title.

I remember a time when the company was going through a major setback. They had a major product launch that tanked, and there was a lot of finger-pointing going on. Most leaders would've tried to cover it up, sweep it under the rug, or place blame on the team. Not Sarah. She came into the meeting and said, "This is a mess. But you know what? It's my mess. I made decisions that led us here, and I'm going to fix it. Let's figure this out together."

She didn't have all the answers right then and there. She didn't pretend like everything was fine. But she did something that very few leaders do—she took ownership, and she showed vulnerability. She didn't act like some distant authority figure who had all the answers. She was a leader who was willing to admit she didn't know it all, but was committed to figuring it out with her team. People respected that. People followed her because she wasn't afraid to be human.

The most powerful part of this? After that meeting, people weren't afraid to come to her with their ideas, their mistakes, or their concerns. They knew she'd listen. They knew she wouldn't judge them. She'd help them learn and grow. And that's what a great leader does—they create a space where people feel safe to be themselves. They build trust. They build loyalty. And you can't build any of that if you're hiding behind a mask.

I've seen this same pattern with countless leaders I've coached over the years. The ones who try to be something they're not—who push the whole 'perfect leader' act—are the ones who fall flat. The ones who show up as themselves, who lead with empathy, authenticity, and a willingness to be human—those are the ones who inspire real loyalty and build high-performing teams.

But I get it. You're probably thinking, "But I don't want to seem weak. I don't want to be seen as incompetent." Well, let me tell you something—vulnerability is not weakness. Vulnerability is strength. It takes guts to admit you don't have all the answers, to ask for help, to show empathy. It takes courage to be honest with your team about what's going wrong and how you're going to fix it. That's what makes people trust you. That's what makes people believe in you. And that's what inspires them to work all out for you.

Now, I'm not saying you should abandon all professional boundaries and act like you're best friends with every person on your team. No. But don't be afraid to show that you're human. Share your struggles. Acknowledge your mistakes. Don't try to be some infallible figure who can never show weakness. People see right through that, and it'll cost you in the long run.

So, here's your challenge: drop the corporate façade. Stop pretending to be perfect. Show up as you—flaws and all. Lead with humanity. Lead with emotion. Lead with authenticity. And watch how your team responds. They'll respect you more. They'll follow you more. And they'll give you everything they've got. Because that's what great leadership is about. Being real. Being human. And building connections that last.

So, if you're ready to be an awesome boss, stop hiding behind the robot mask. Lead like a human. That's the difference between mediocrity and greatness. Make it happen.

Strategy 10 – Build Leaders, Not Followers

If you're in a leadership role and you're just creating followers, you're doing it wrong. You're failing. And here's why—your job isn't to build a loyal fan club or a group of people who just follow orders. Your job is to build other leaders. Leaders who can think for themselves, make decisions, and take the reins when you're not around.

Let that sink in. If you're hoarding all the power, all the ideas, and all the control, you're not building anything. You're creating a bottleneck. You're creating a team that's completely dependent on you, and that's a disaster waiting to happen. The day you leave, everything will crumble. You won't be remembered for your achievements; you'll be remembered for running a dictatorship, not a team.

Here's the crunch: being a leader isn't about making everyone else follow your lead. It's about teaching them to lead. When you build leaders, you create a self-sustaining team. You create a legacy. You create a culture where people don't just execute—they innovate. They make decisions. They own their results. And ultimately, that's what sets great bosses apart from the mediocre ones. Mediocre bosses build followers. Great bosses build leaders.

I've seen this happen time and time again with the best leaders. One example that stands out in my mind is a senior executive I worked with named Tim. Tim was a leader who understood this concept on a deep level. He didn't want a team of yes-men or people who only followed his instructions. He wanted people who could think for themselves, challenge the status quo, and take initiative.

One of the most profound things Tim did as a leader was give his team room to fail. And I'm not talking about some soft, "Oh, it's okay to make mistakes" kind of talk. No. Tim created an environment where his people could take risks, learn from their failures, and come back stronger. He'd ask questions like, "What did you learn from that?" or "How would you handle this next time?" He never treated failure as a death sentence. He treated it as a stepping stone.

And you know what? His team started thinking like leaders. They started taking ownership of their work. They started stepping up to challenges, even when it wasn't easy. Tim's focus was never on micromanaging; it was on enabling. Enabling his team to make decisions. Enabling them to lead. Enabling them to grow into better versions of themselves. And in turn, his organization became a powerhouse, full of people who were not just carrying out orders but actively driving the business forward.

But here's the problem most leaders face: they're terrified of losing control. They're scared of empowering their teams because they think their authority will slip away. They think, "If I don't have all the answers, or if my team starts making their own decisions, what's left for me?" Let me break it to you: it's the exact opposite. When you build leaders, you create more freedom, more creativity, and more ownership. When people take ownership of their work, they take pride in it. They care. And when they care, the results speak for themselves.

So, stop being a bottleneck. Stop being the only one with all the answers. Start creating a team of leaders who can take the reins, make decisions, and lead in their own right. When you create leaders, you don't have to worry about "what happens when I'm gone." The system you've built will carry on, and it will thrive. And you'll be remembered as the boss who built something sustainable, not the one who hoarded all the power.

THE AWESOME BOSS PLAYBOOK: 10 STRATEGIES FOR LEADING WITH STYLE

I can already hear the objections: "But I can't trust them. They might mess things up." News flash—people will mess up. That's part of the process. If you're trying to prevent mistakes at all costs, you're limiting growth. You're stifling innovation. It's not about avoiding failure—it's about managing it and learning from it. Your team isn't going to become great leaders if you don't let them fail occasionally. Don't create a culture of perfectionism. Create a culture of learning. Encourage your team to take ownership of their decisions, whether they succeed or fail. They'll learn more from their failures than from their successes.

Look, I'm not saying you need to completely step out of the way and let your team run wild. No one is advocating for chaos here. But you've got to create an environment where leadership can flourish. You need to be willing to delegate, to trust your team, and to give them the space to grow. If you can't do that, you'll be stuck managing a group of people who never exceed their potential. And that's not just a failure for them—it's a failure for you.

You want to be remembered as an awesome boss? Start building leaders. Invest in your people. Develop their skills. Teach them how to lead, how to make decisions, and how to handle challenges. When you do that, you create a team that's not only self-sufficient, but also driven to achieve even more. They'll have your back, not because they have to, but because they want to. And that's a powerful thing.

I've seen the power of this principle firsthand. When you build leaders, you create a culture of ownership and accountability. You create a group of people who don't just work for you—they work for themselves. They're motivated, they're engaged, and they're driven. And when your team is motivated and engaged, there's nothing they can't accomplish. So stop leading like a boss and start leading like a coach, a mentor, a developer of leaders. When you do that, the results will speak for themselves.

The bottom line? Leadership isn't about creating followers. It's about creating leaders. So go out there, empower your team, and watch them soar. That's the true mark of a great boss.

Conclusion – The Time to Lead Is Now

Well, here we are—at the end of the playbook. You've just walked through 10 strategies that can help you become the kind of boss people talk about with respect, admiration, and even a little awe. But let me tell you something: reading this book, nodding along, and thinking "Yeah, that sounds good" isn't going to cut it. The real work starts now.

If you're serious about being an awesome boss, it's not just about knowing the strategies. It's about implementing them. Day in, day out. And trust me, it's not going to be easy. Leading with style means taking risks, making tough decisions, and showing up for your people in ways that require more than just a title on your business card.

You can't just read this book and expect magic to happen. The strategies in here? They're only as good as your ability to make them part of your daily routine. So, let's take a moment to recap what we've covered, and I'll leave you with a call to action to really step up.

Recap: The Power of Leading with Style

1. **Be the Lighthouse, Not the Spotlight**
   It's not about you. Period. Your job is to guide, not to outshine. Be the steady hand, the calm in the storm. Let your team feel like they're the ones making things happen, while you quietly lead them from behind. You're the lighthouse, not the spotlight.

THE AWESOME BOSS PLAYBOOK: 10 STRATEGIES FOR LEADING WITH STYLE

2. Hire Smart, Then Get Out of Their Way
   You don't have to be the smartest person in the room. You just have to know how to hire the smartest people, then let them do their thing. Micromanaging is dead. Empower your people, give them the tools they need, and get out of their way.
3. Say It Like You Mean It
   Drop the corporate fluff. Speak plainly, even when it's uncomfortable. People respect straight talk. If you can't say what's on your mind, you're not leading—you're avoiding. Be real, even when the truth stings.
4. Feedback: Give It, Take It, Love It
   Don't just give feedback—learn how to take it. Feedback is a two-way street, and if you can't handle it, then how can you expect your team to? Be a coach, not a critic.
5. Celebrate Wins, Fix the Fails
   Cheer loud for victories. Own up to mistakes. When things go south, don't play the blame game. Fix the problem, learn from it, and move on. You'll build a team that's resilient, accountable, and ready for anything.
6. Master the Art of the Coffee Chat
   Don't be the boss who only talks to their people during meetings. Grab coffee, sit down, and actually listen. Find out what drives them, what challenges them, what they want to achieve. The best leaders know their people.
7. Be the Calm in the Chaos
   When everything goes kaput, your team will look to you. If you're freaking out, they will too. Stay calm, keep your head, and show them how to handle pressure. Leaders don't crack under stress; they make sure the team doesn't crack either.
8. Decisions: Make Them, Own Them
   Indecision is poison to a team. You can't sit on the fence all the time. Make decisions, own them, and move forward. Even if it's

the wrong decision, it's better than making no decision at all. Own your choices, good or bad.
9. Lead Like a Human, Not a Robot
People don't connect with robots. They connect with humans. Show some emotion. Crack a joke. Admit when you're wrong. Be authentic. That's how you build loyalty.
10. Build Leaders, Not Followers
This is the big one, the game-changer. Don't create followers—create leaders. Give your people the tools, the confidence, and the freedom to lead themselves. The best bosses build leaders who can run the show when they're not around.

The Hard Truth

If you've made it this far and you're still feeling fired up, then you're ready to take the next step. But here's the hard truth: none of this will work if you don't commit. If you think you can breeze through this and then keep doing things the way you always have, you're wrong. These strategies demand action. They require change. And change is uncomfortable. But that's where growth happens.

You can't be the boss who just sits in the corner office, barking orders and hoping for results. You have to show up every single day with purpose, with energy, and with the drive to do better—for yourself and for your team.

Your Call to Action

So here's my challenge to you: Stop thinking about being a boss. Start thinking about being a leader. You've got the strategies. Now, it's time to take action. And if you mess up? Good. Learn from it. Adjust, adapt, and keep going. The best leaders aren't the ones who avoid mistakes; they're the ones who rise after every fall.

The world doesn't need another average boss. It doesn't need another micromanaging, power-hungry figurehead. What it needs is someone who's willing to step up, lead with heart, and build other leaders along the way. The world needs more awesome bosses. And I'm calling on you to be one of them.

So, what are you waiting for? The time to lead is now. Get out there, put these strategies into action, and start building something real. Your team, your organization, and your legacy will thank you for it. And when people look back on your leadership, they'll say, "That boss? They changed everything."

Let's make that happen.

About the Author

Marako Marcus is a management consultant, coach, and public speaker with over 25 years of experience, and a reputation for being straight to the point. He helps executives, teams, and individuals face their challenges head-on, cutting through the corporate nonsense and delivering results that matter. With years of experience working with organizations of all sizes, Marako has knowledge of what's wrong with most workplaces and ideas on how to fix them—without the usual corporate jargon.

A master of tough love and tough conversations, he's a coach who asks those powerful questions, tells it like it is and makes sure you know exactly where you stand. His approach is simple: if you're not getting it done, stop whining and start acting. He's worked with leaders who need a wake-up call and teams who need someone to light a fire under them.

When he's not stirring up success in the business world, Marako unleashes his creativity as a musician and producer. Yes, he's the guy who can juggle spreadsheets and compose a killer track at the same time—proving that sharp focus can strike the right chord in both the boardroom and the studio. Marako's blend of directness and creativity makes him a unique voice in the business world—and someone you'll want to listen to.

Read more at https://linktr.ee/marakomarcusbooks.

www.ingramcontent.com/pod-product-compliance
Lightning Source LLC
Chambersburg PA
CBHW070420230526
45471CB00006B/2892